FIRST 50
PIANO SOLOS

YOU SHOULD PLAY

ISBN 978-1-70513-698-0

Visit Hal Leonard Online at
www.halleonard.com

World headquarters, contact:
Hal Leonard
7777 West Bluemound Road
Milwaukee, WI 53213
Email: info@halleonard.com

In Europe, contact:
Hal Leonard Europe Limited
1 Red Place
London, W1K 6PL
Email: info@halleonardeurope.com

In Australia, contact:
Hal Leonard Australia Pty. Ltd.
4 Lentara Court
Cheltenham, Victoria, 3192 Australia
Email: info@halleonard.com.au

CONTENTS

ALWAYS

Words and Music by
IRVING BERLIN

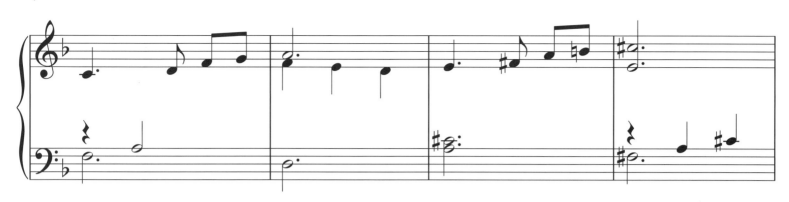

ALL OF ME

By JON SCHMIDT'

Freely, like a fanfare

With pedal

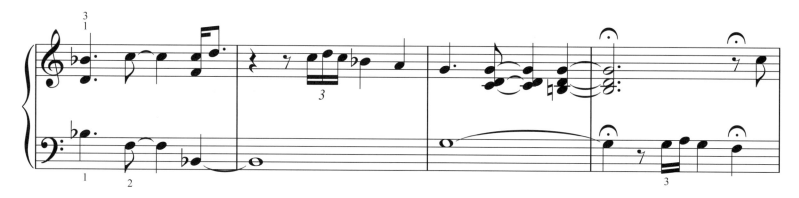

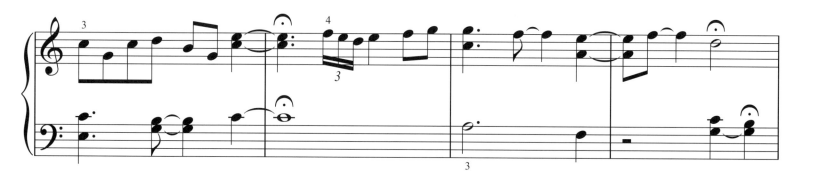

Fast (put "all of yourself" into it)

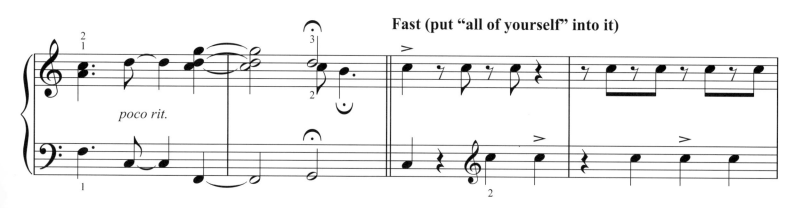

poco rit.

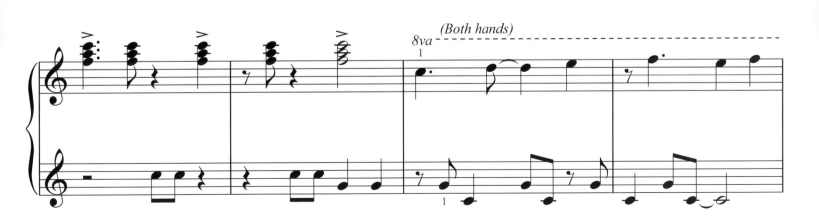

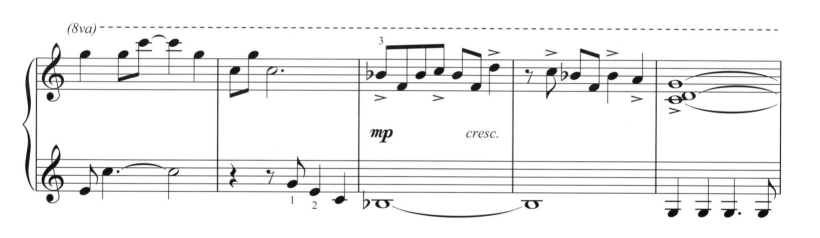

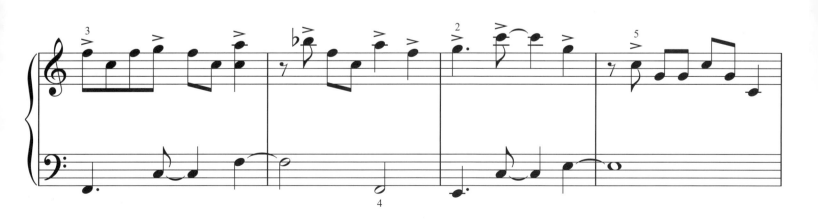

molto cresc.

ff

ALL THE THINGS YOU ARE
from VERY WARM FOR MAY

Lyrics by OSCAR HAMMERSTEIN II
Music by JEROME KERN

Slowly, expressively

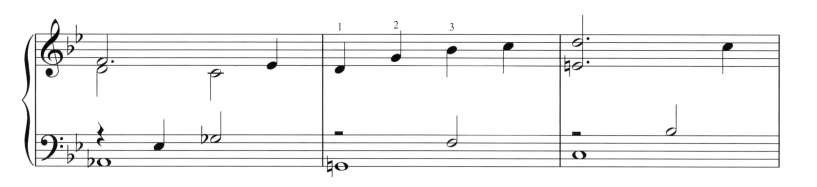

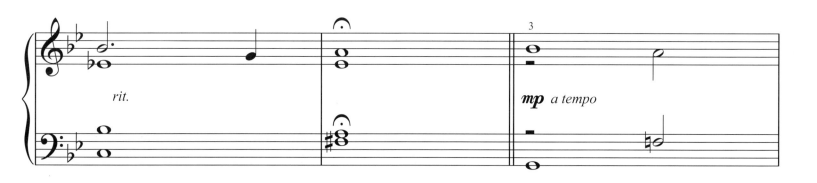

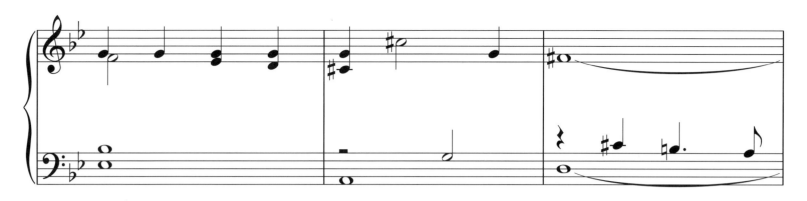

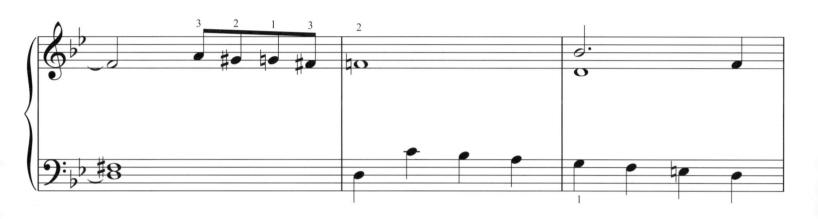

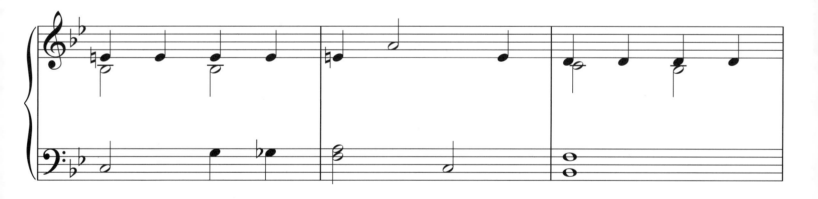

ARIETTA IN C MAJOR

from AN INTRODUCTION TO THE ART OF PLAYING ON THE PIANOFORTE, OP. 42

By MUZIO CLEMENTI

Allegretto

AT THE IVY GATE

By BRIAN CRAIN

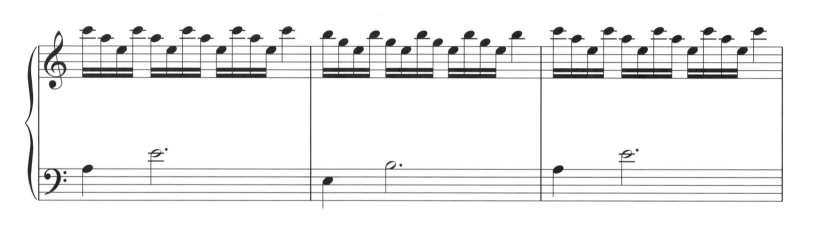

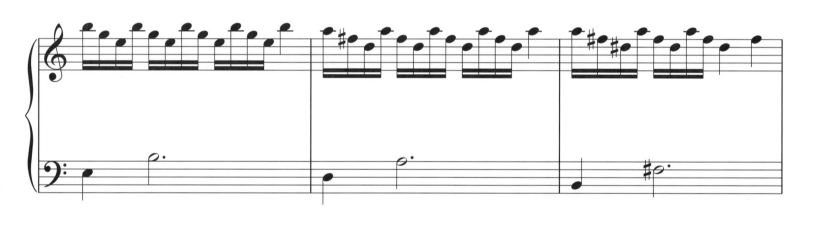

BABY ELEPHANT WALK

from the Paramount Picture HATARI!

Words by HAL DAVID
Music by HENRY MANCINI

Moderately slow and steady

sempre staccato

THE CIDER HOUSE RULES
(Main Titles)
from the Miramax Motion Picture THE CIDER HOUSE RULES

By RACHEL PORTMAN

Moderately

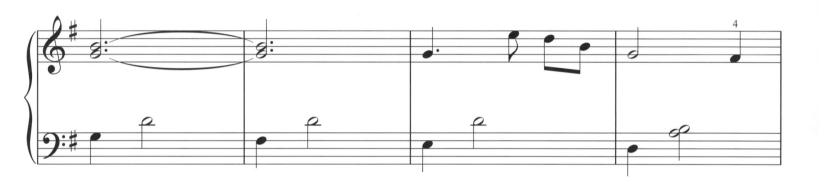

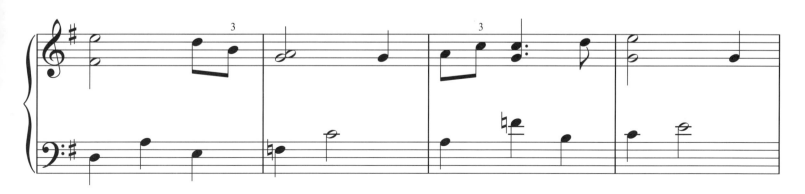

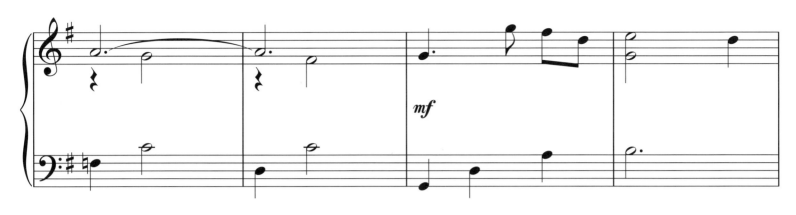

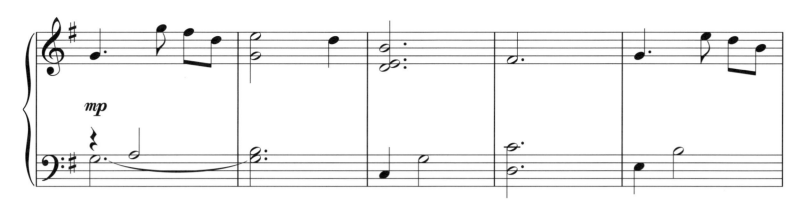

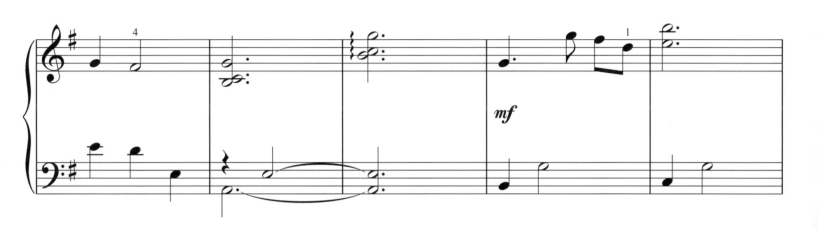

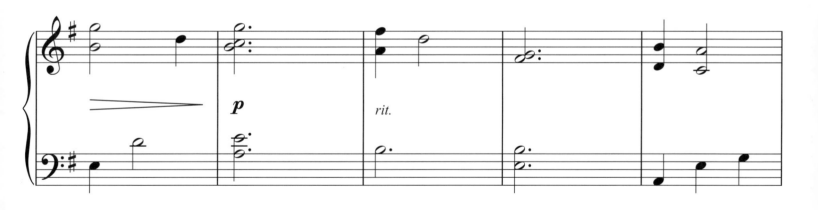

CITY OF STARS

from LA LA LAND

Music by JUSTIN HURWITZ
Lyrics by BENJ PASEK & JUSTIN PAUL

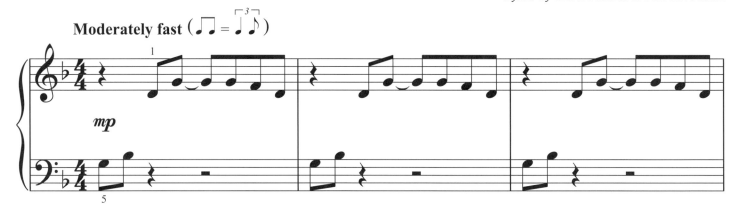

31

CLAIR DE LUNE

By CLAUDE DEBUSSY

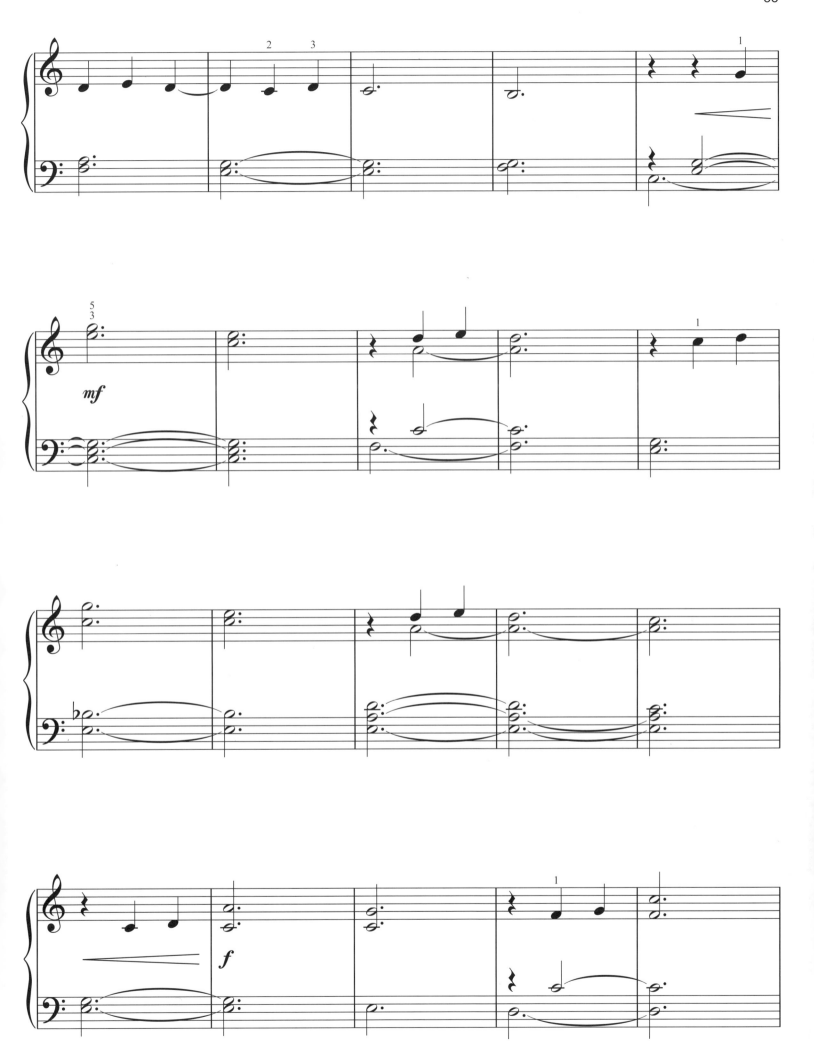

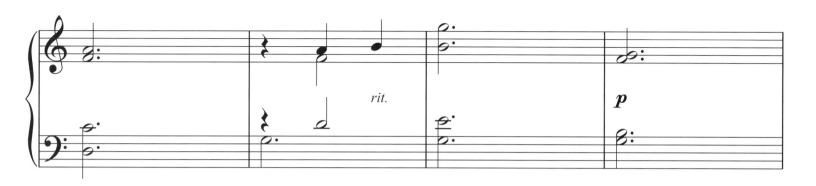

COME RAIN OR COME SHINE
from ST. LOUIS WOMAN

Words by JOHNNY MERCER
Music by HAROLD ARLEN

Moderately slow, bluesy

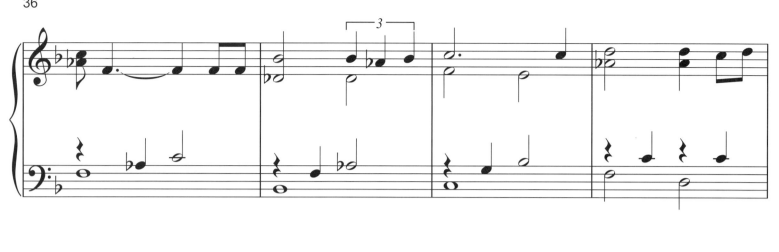

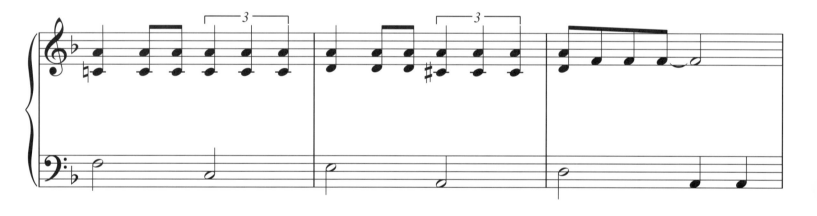

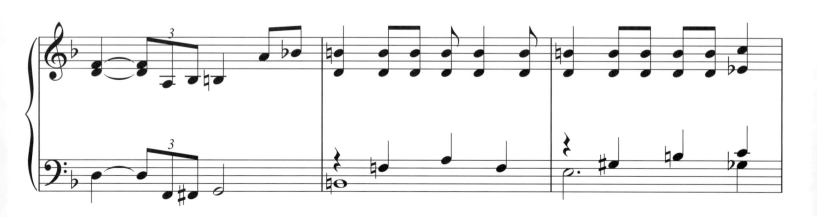

COMPTINE D'UN AUTRE ÉTÉ: L'APRÈS-MIDI
from AMÉLIE

By YANN TIERSEN

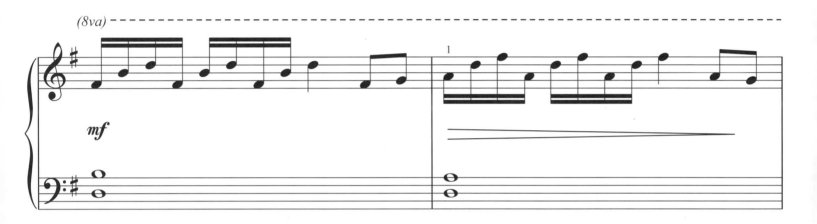

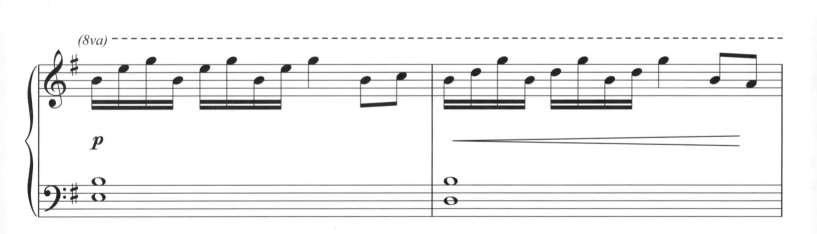

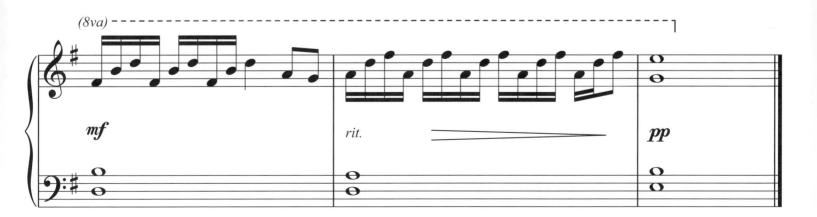

CONSOLATION NO. 3

By FRANZ LISZT

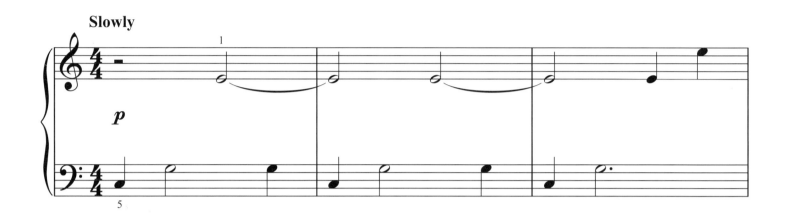

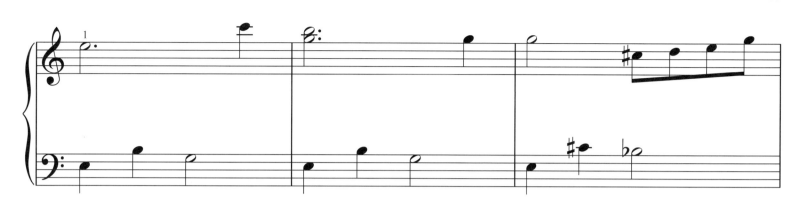

rit.

THE ENTERTAINER

By SCOTT JOPLIN

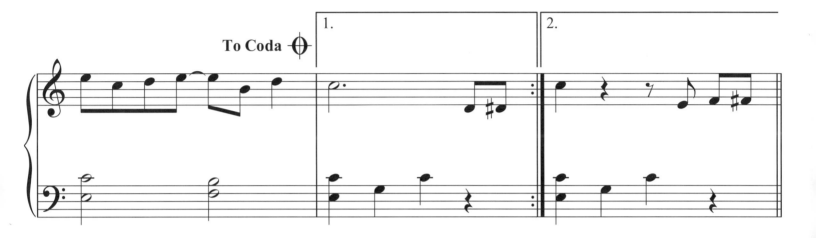

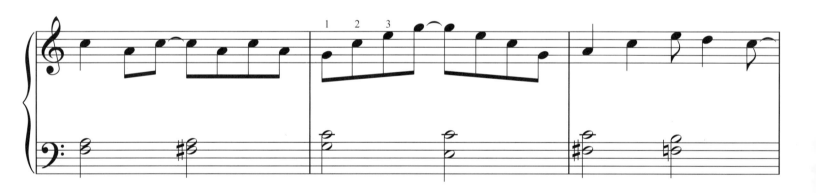

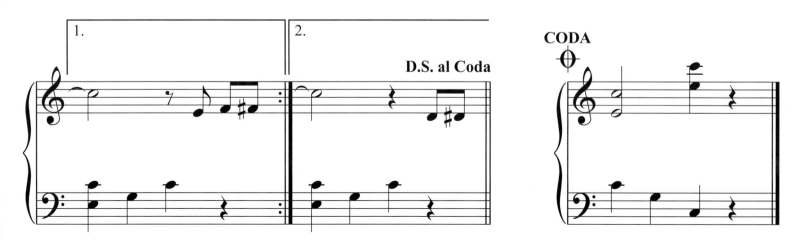

FALLIN'

Words and Music by
ALICIA KEYS

Moderate Blues tempo

FOR THE LOVE OF A PRINCESS

from the Twentieth Century Fox Motion Picture BRAVEHEART

Music by JAMES HORNER

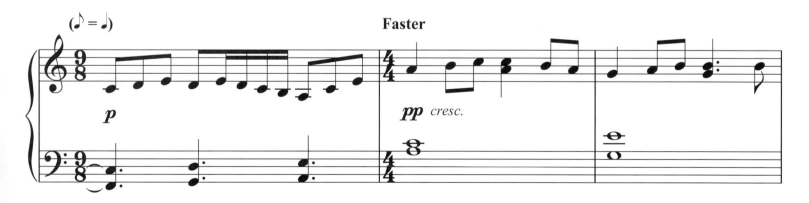

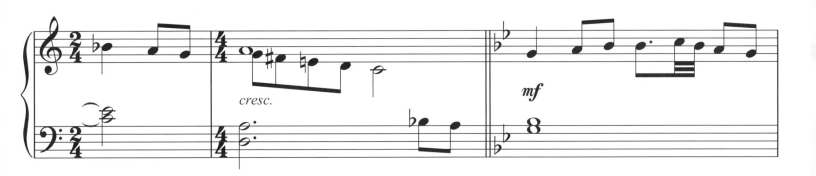

THE GIRL WITH THE FLAXEN HAIR

(La fille aux cheveux de lin)
from PRELUDES, Book 1

By CLAUDE DEBUSSY

Calm, with expression

With pedal

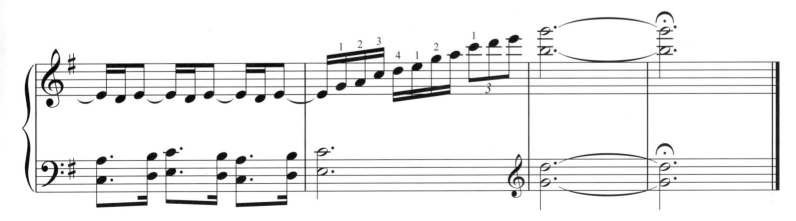

HEART AND SOUL
from the Paramount Short Subject A SONG IS BORN

Words by FRANK LOESSER
Music by HOAGY CARMICHAEL

HYMN

By LIZ STORY

Moderately

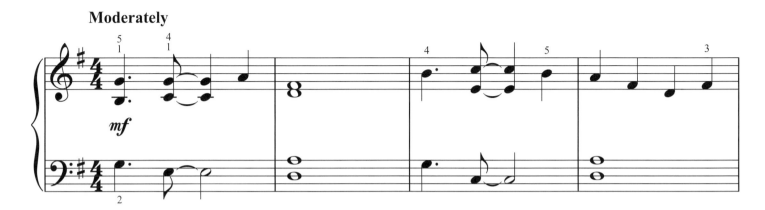

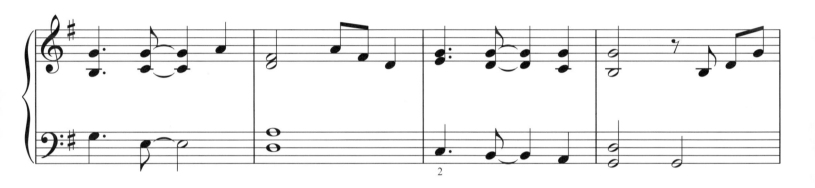

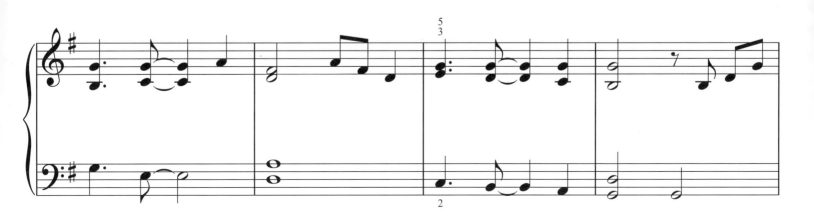

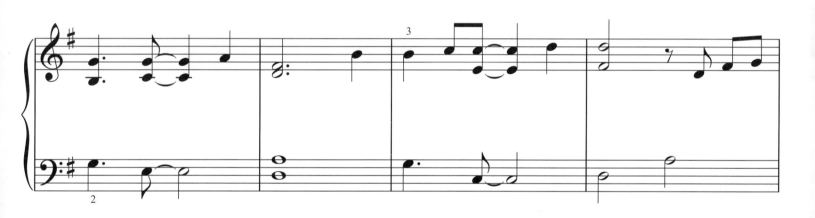

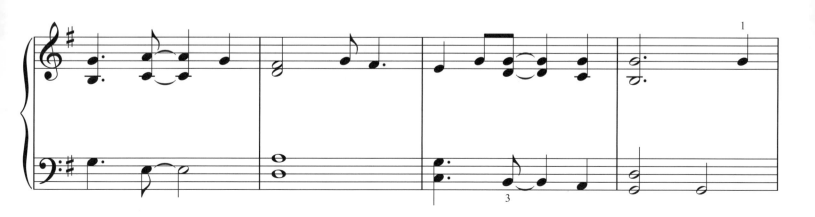

IMAGINE

Words and Music by
JOHN LENNON

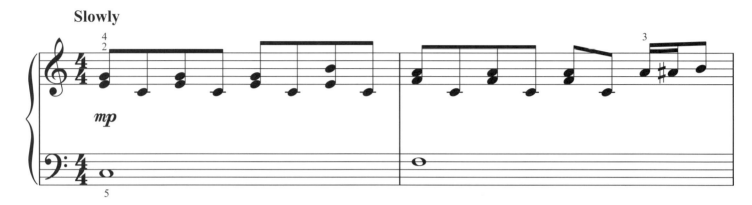

IN FLIGHT

By MICHAEL HARRISON

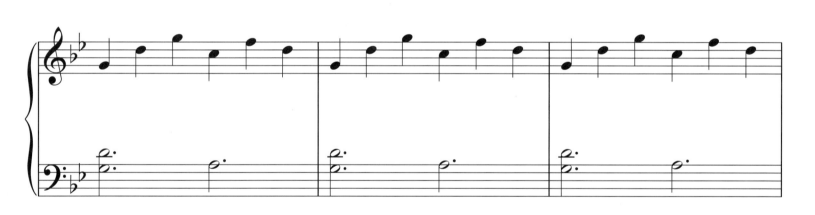

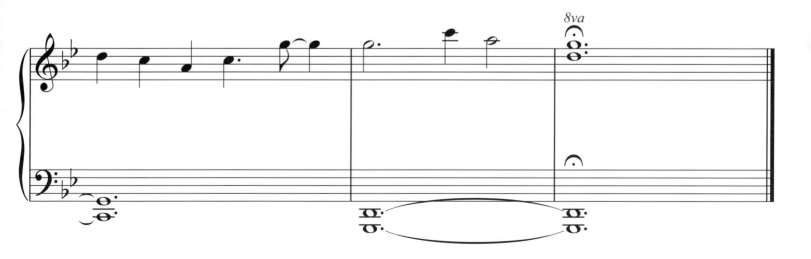

LEAN ON ME

Words and Music by
BILL WITHERS

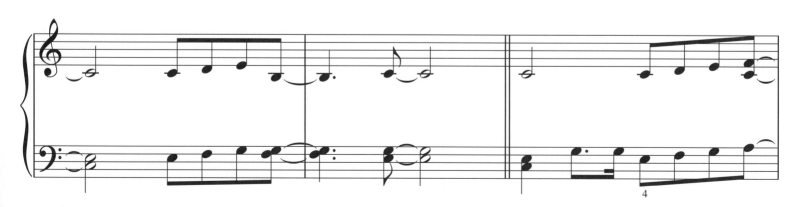

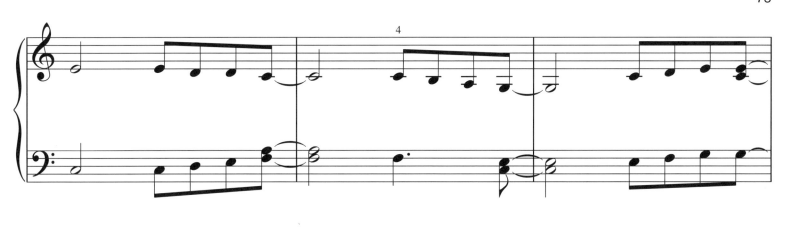

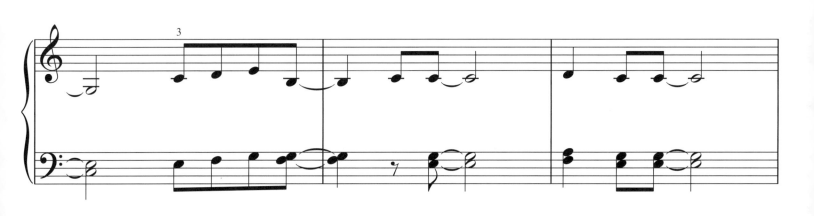

LET IT BE

Words and Music by JOHN LENNON
and PAUL McCARTNEY

Moderately slow

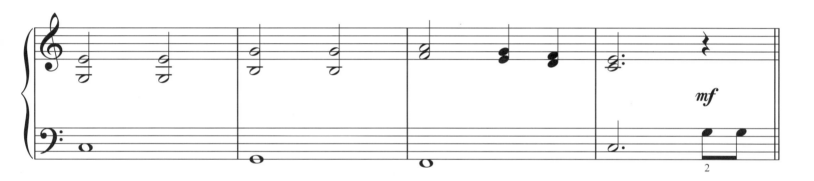

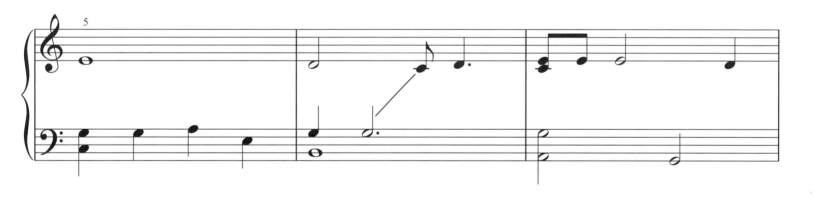

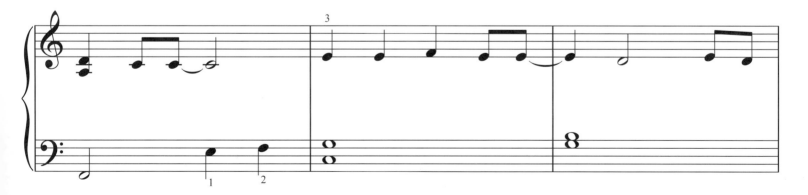

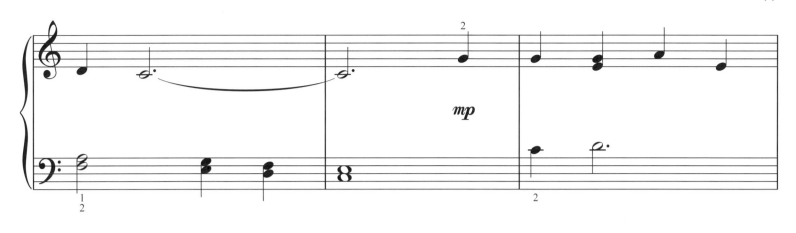

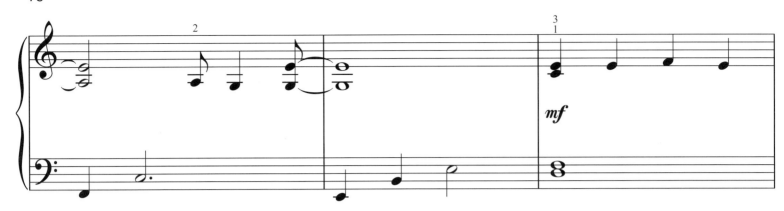

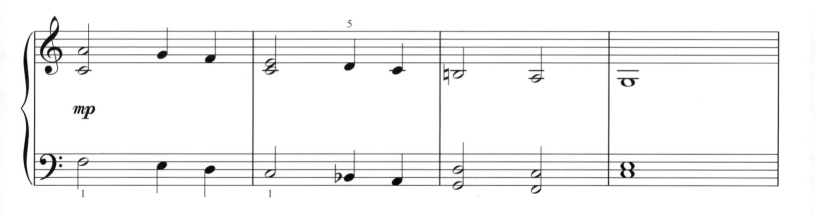

LINUS AND LUCY

from A CHARLIE BROWN CHRISTMAS

By VINCE GUARALDI

MISTY

Words by JOHNNY BURKE
Music by ERROLL GARNER

Moderately slow, freely

LULLABY OF BIRDLAND

Words by GEORGE DAVID WEISS
Music by GEORGE SHEARING

Moderate Swing

MARRIED LIFE

from UP

By MICHAEL GIACCHINO

Moderately fast

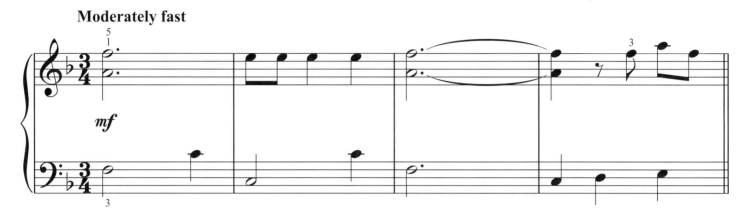

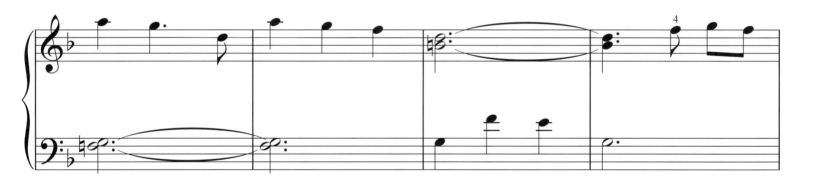

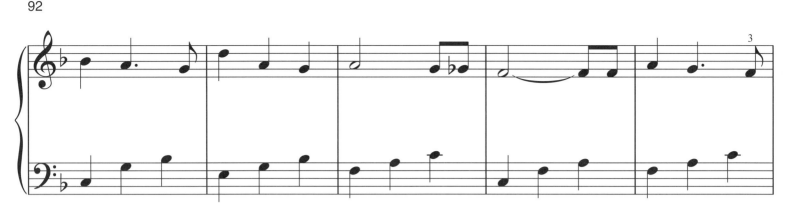

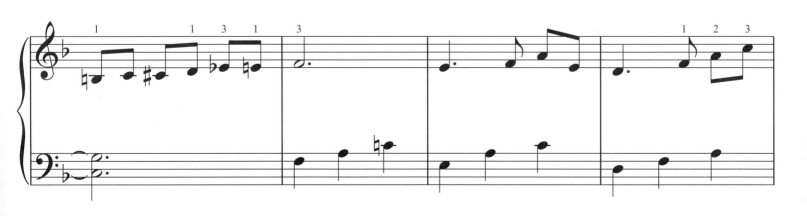

MOON RIVER
from the Paramount Picture BREAKFAST AT TIFFANY'S

Words by JOHNNY MERCER
Music by HENRY MANCINI

Moderately slow

"MOONLIGHT" SONATA
(First Movement Theme)

By LUDWIG VAN BEETHOVEN

Adagio sostenuto

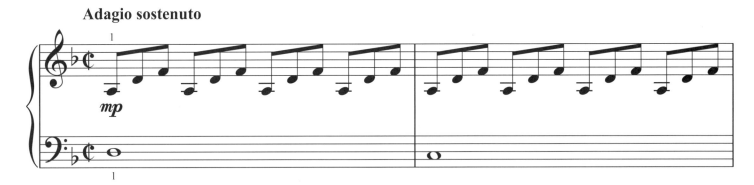

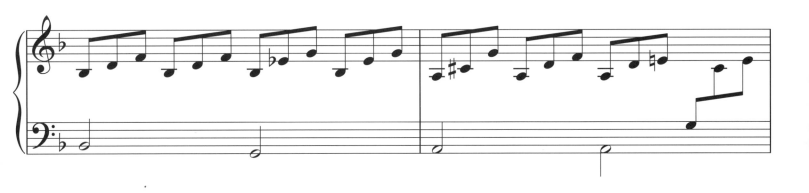

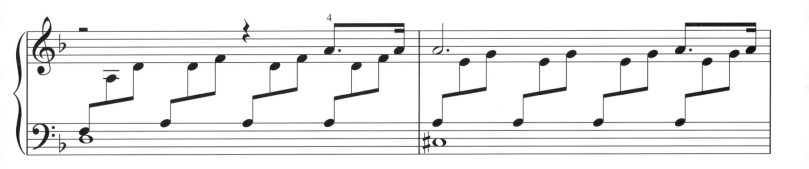

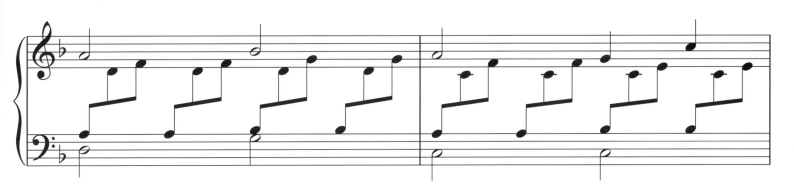

NOCTURNE IN E-FLAT MAJOR
Op. 9, No. 2

By FRÉDÉRIC CHOPIN

Slowly, in 1

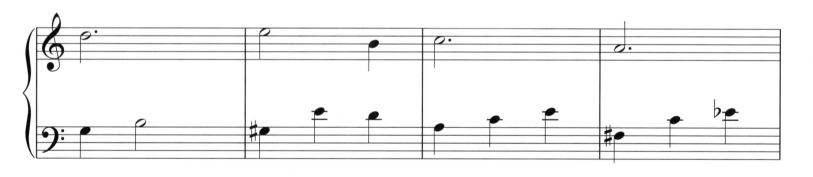

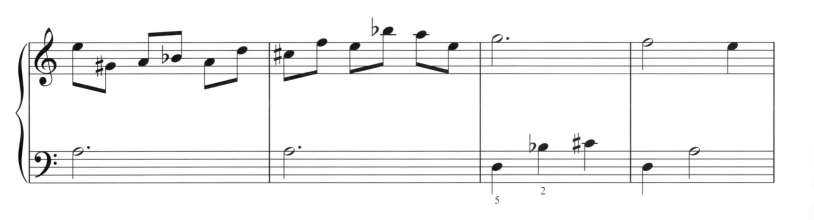

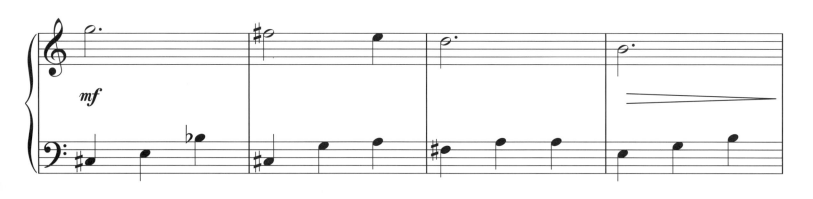

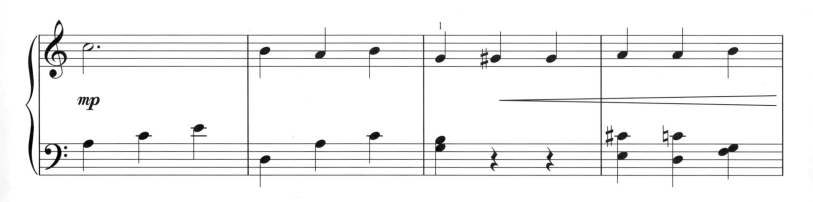

NOTHING FROM NOTHING

Words and Music by BILLY PRESTON
and BRUCE FISHER

Energetically, in 2

ONE LAST WISH

from CASPER

By JAMES HORNER

Moderately

mp

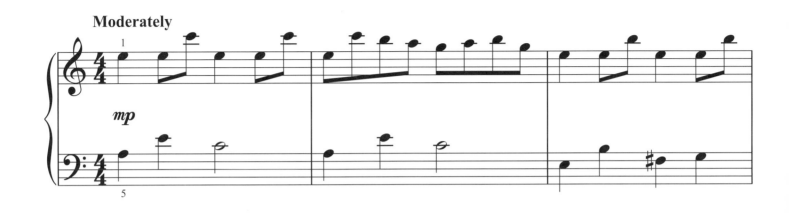

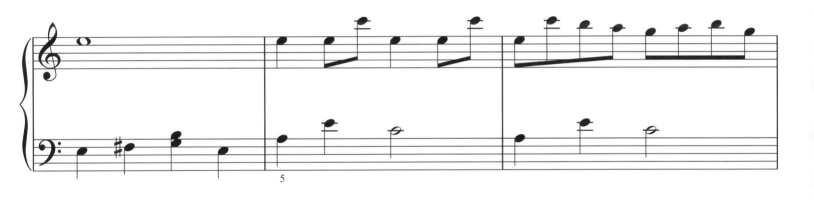

a tempo

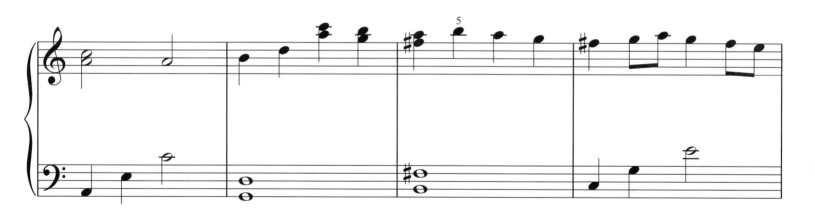

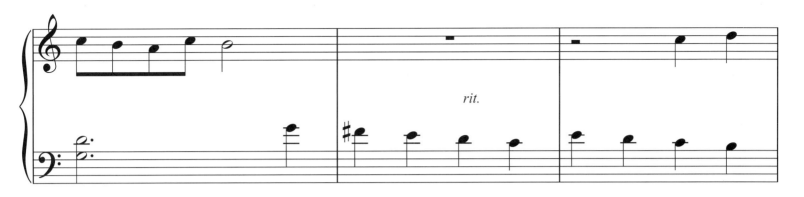

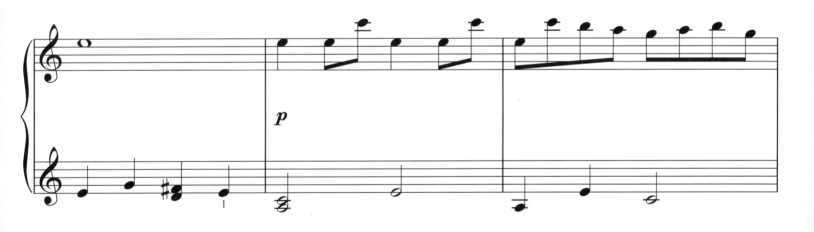

ONE SUMMER'S DAY
from SPIRITED AWAY

By JOE HISAISHI

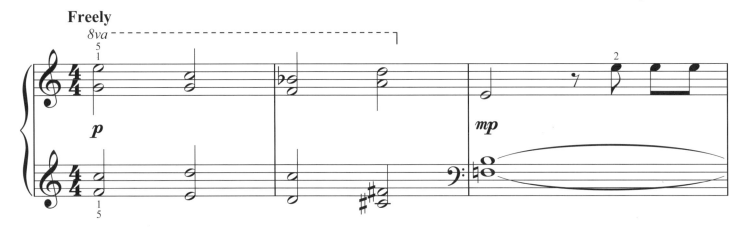

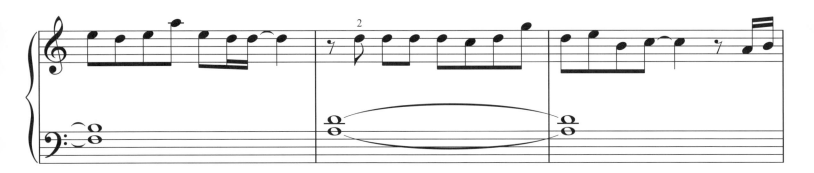

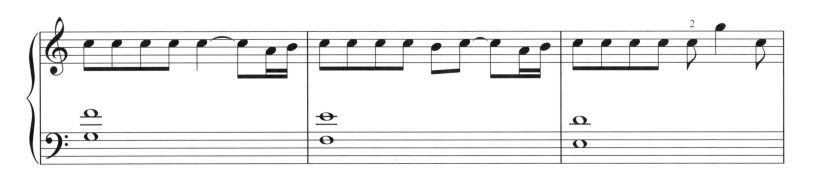

PIANO MAN

Words and Music by
BILLY JOEL

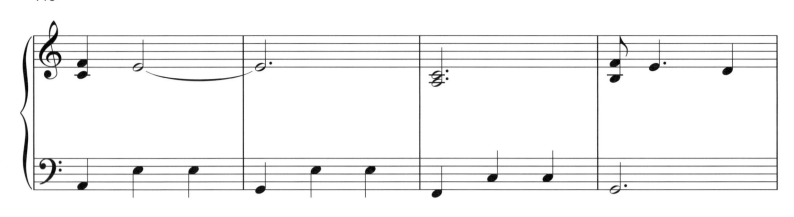

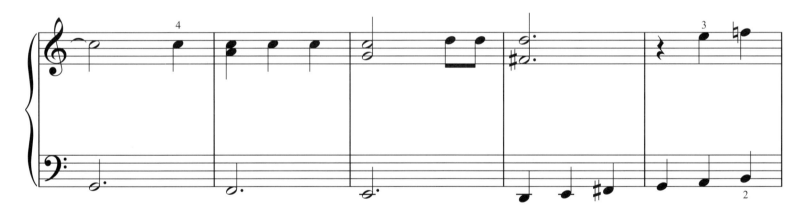

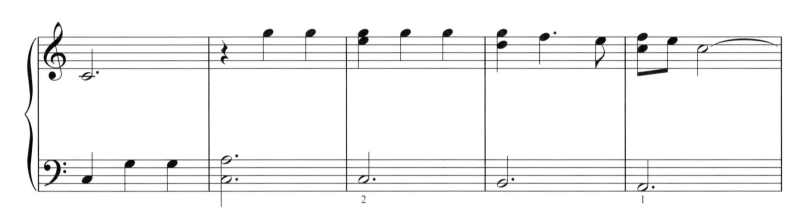

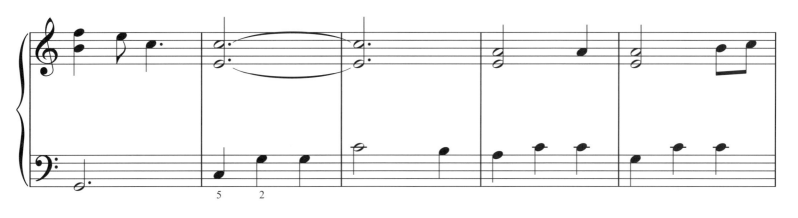

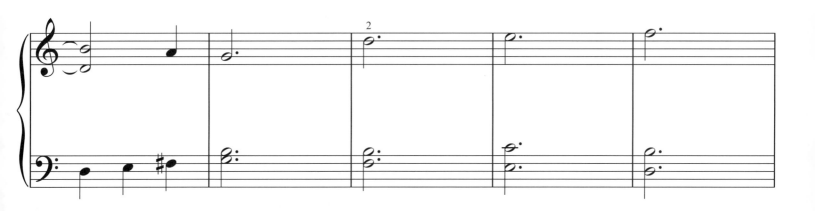

PIANO SONATA NO. 8 "PATHETIQUE"

Second Movement

from PIANO SONATA NO. 8 IN C MINOR, OP. 13

By LUDWIG VAN BEETHOVEN

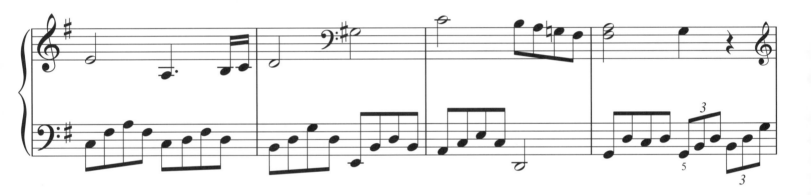

RIVER

Words and Music by
JONI MITCHELL

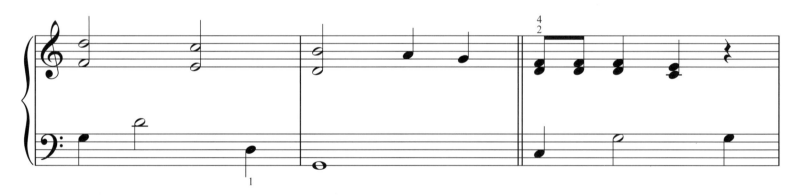

THE PINK PANTHER
from THE PINK PANTHER

By HENRY MANCINI

Moderately, mysteriously

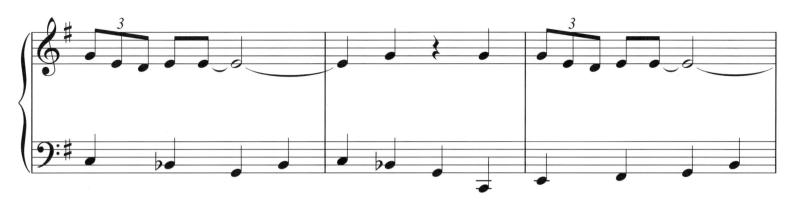

D.S. al Coda

CODA

RHAPSODY IN BLUE

By GEORGE GERSHWIN

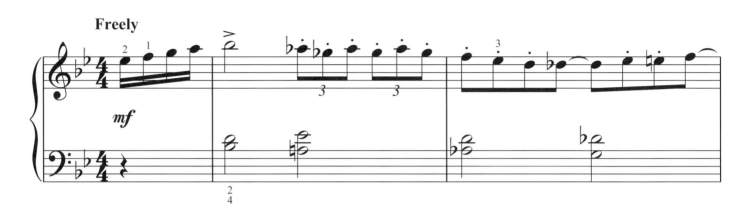

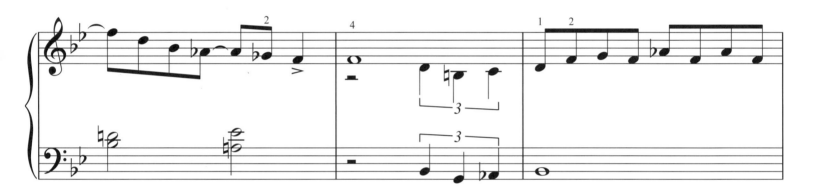

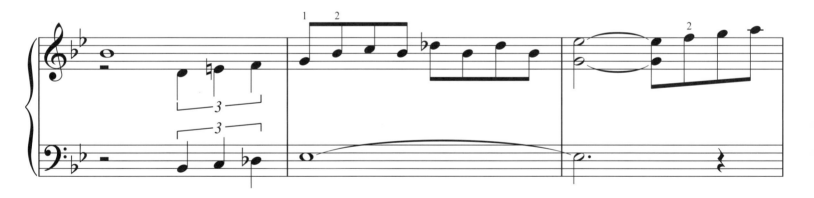

A little faster

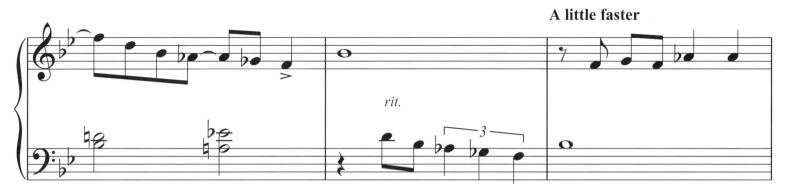

Moderately slow

mp

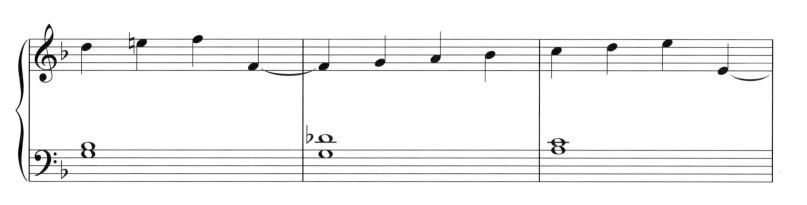

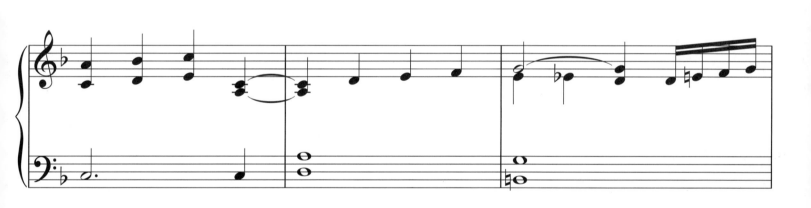

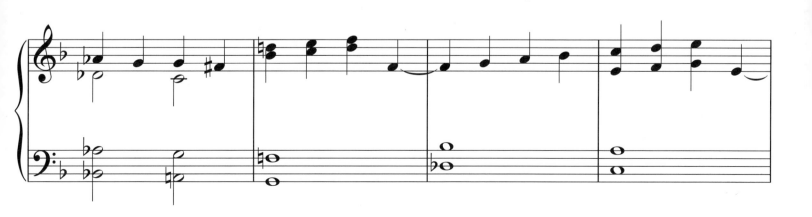

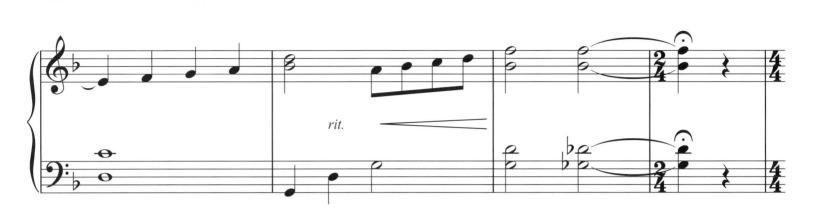

Moderately fast

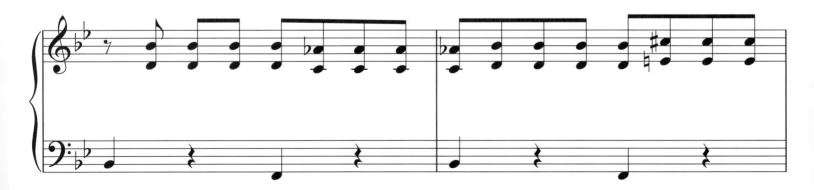

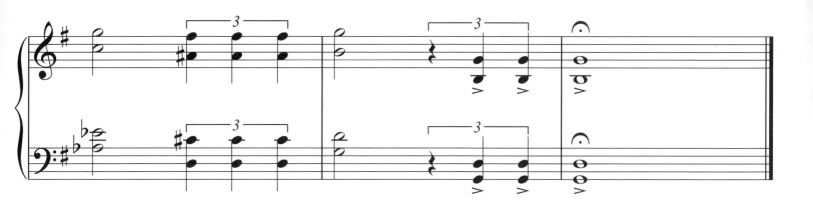

'ROUND MIDNIGHT

Words by BERNIE HANIGHEN
Music by THELONIOUS MONK and COOTIE WILLIAMS

To Coda ⊕

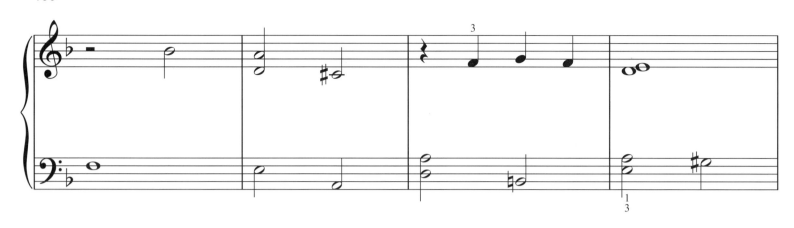

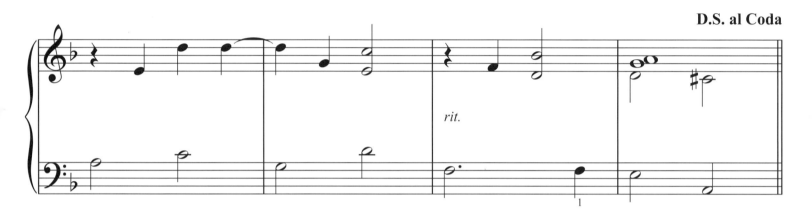

D.S. al Coda

CODA

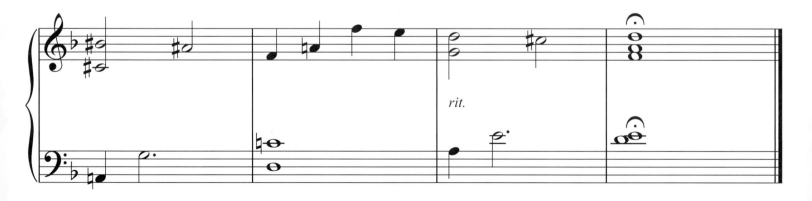

ROMANCES

Music by ZACHARIAS LINDGREN,
OLOF CARL JOHAN OLSON, EMANUEL OLSSON,
ERIK HOLMBERG and ANDERS PETTERSON

Flowing, with feeling

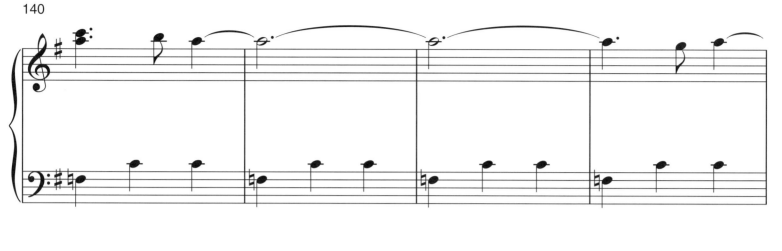

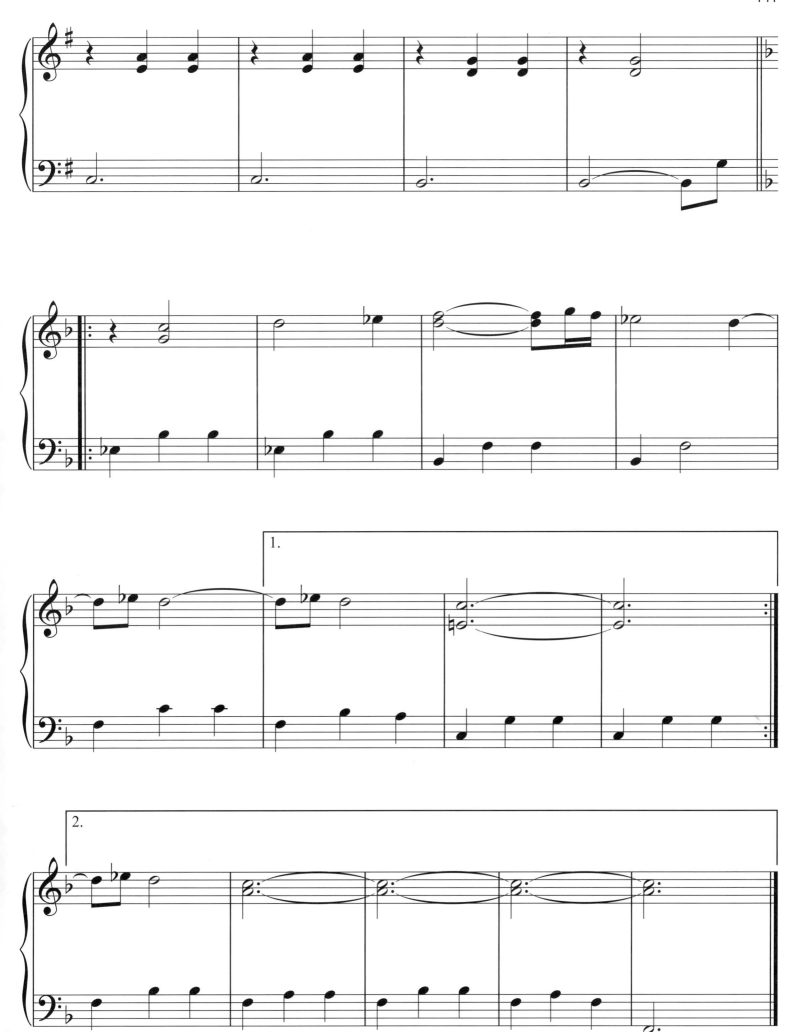

RONDO IN C MAJOR

By WOLFGANG AMADEUS MOZART

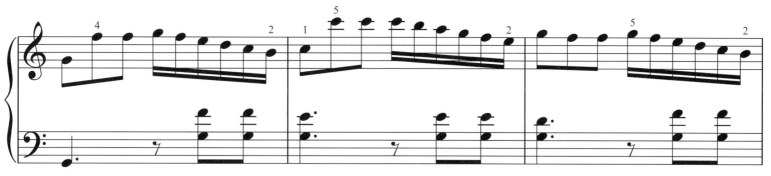

SKATING
from A CHARLIE BROWN CHRISTMAS

By VINCE GUARALDI

Bright Jazz Waltz

D.S. al Coda

CODA

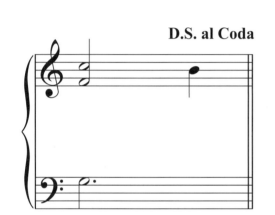

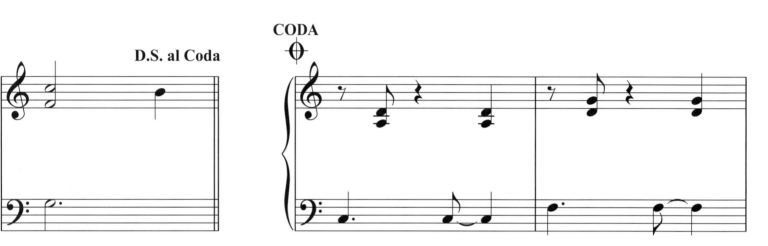

TAKE FIVE

By PAUL DESMOND

149

SOLFEGGIO

By JOHANN CHRISTOPH FRIEDRICH BACH

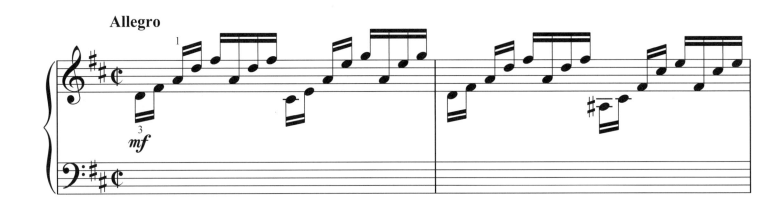

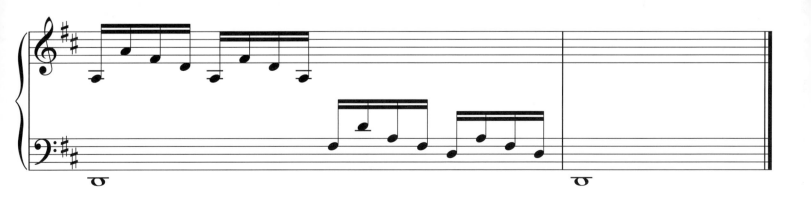

SONG FROM A SECRET GARDEN

By ROLF LOVLAND

Slowly, with expression

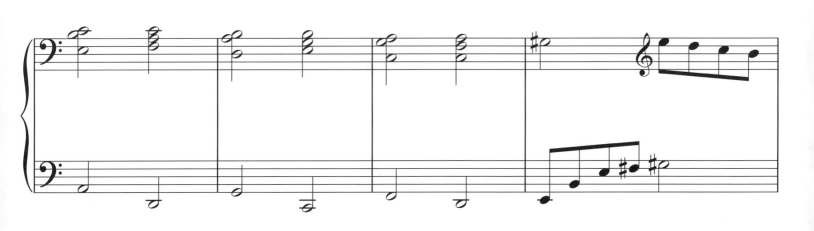

THANKSGIVING
from the solo piano album DECEMBER

By GEORGE WINSTON

Simplified transcription authorized by George Winston.
Full solo transcription found in the Hal Leonard publication GEORGE WINSTON PIANO SOLOS HL00306822.

A THOUSAND YEARS

from the Summit Entertainment film THE TWILIGHT SAGA: BREAKING DAWN - PART 1

Words and Music by DAVID HODGES
and CHRISTINA PERRI

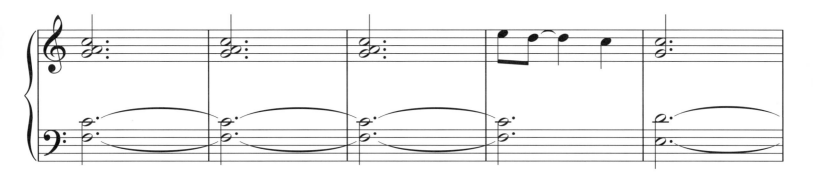

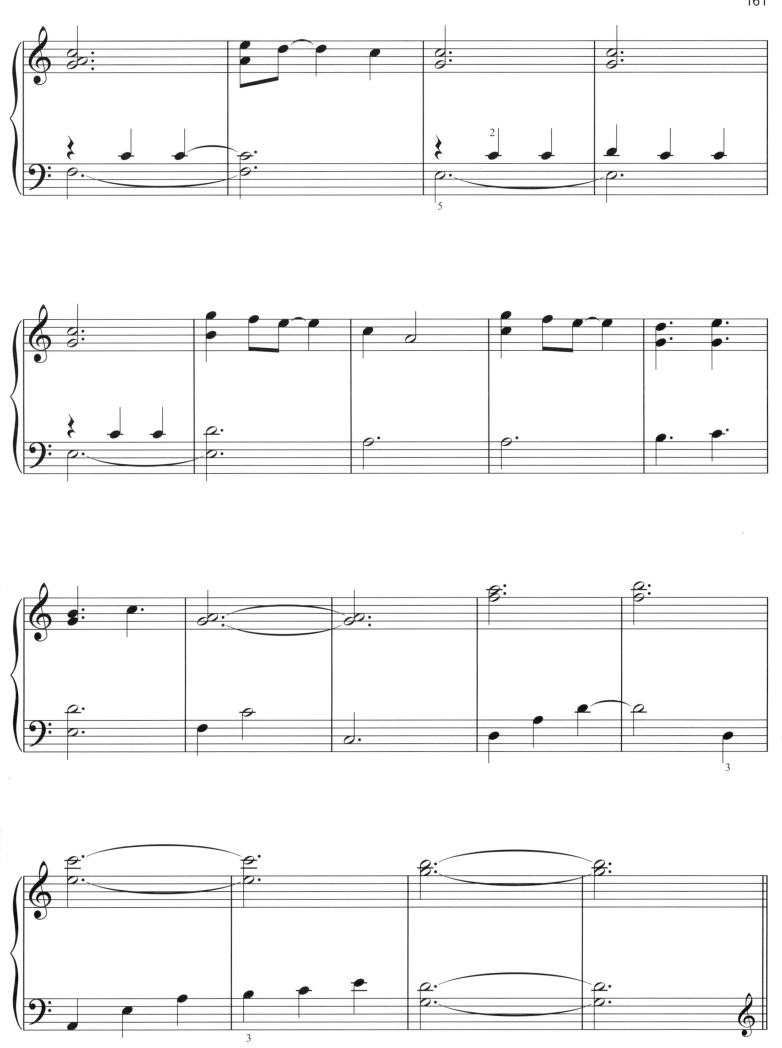

TILL THERE WAS YOU

from Meredith Willson's THE MUSIC MAN

By MEREDITH WILLSON

Freely and expressively

THE WAY YOU LOOK TONIGHT
from SWING TIME

Words by DOROTHY FIELDS
Music by JEROME KERN

Moderate Swing

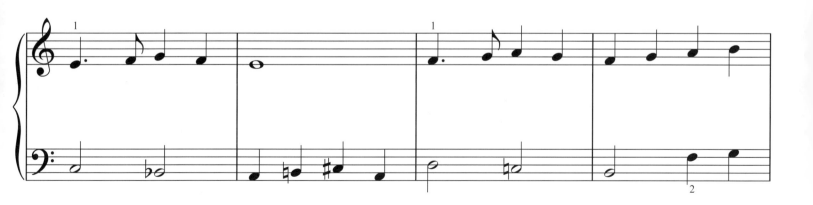

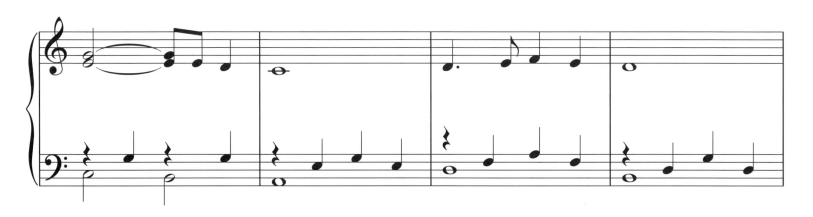

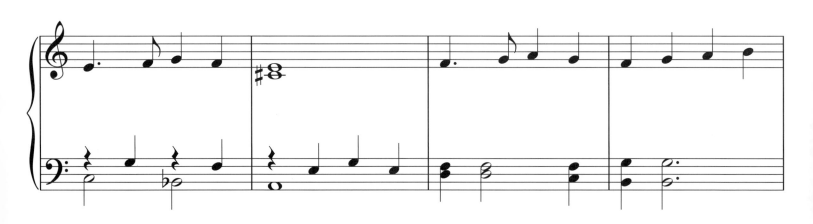

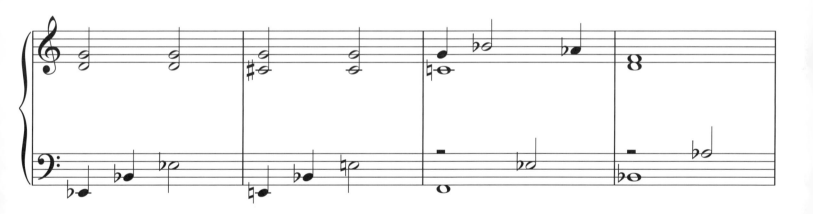

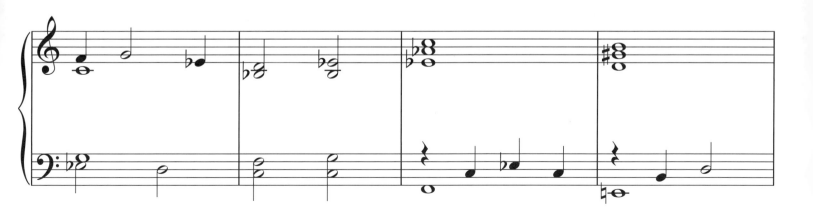

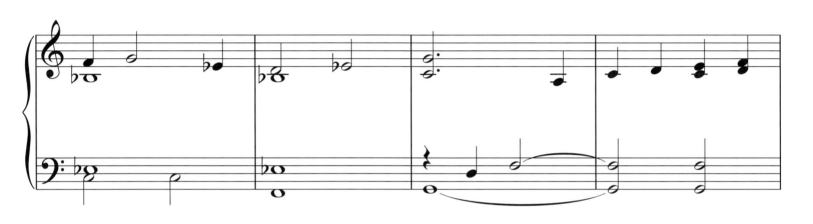

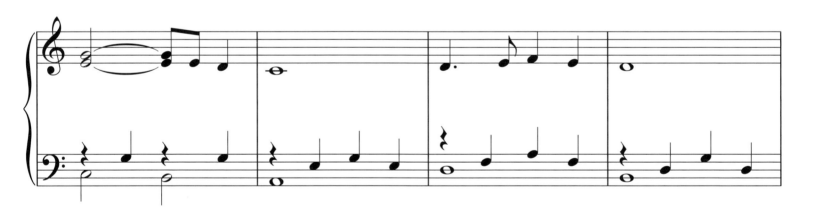

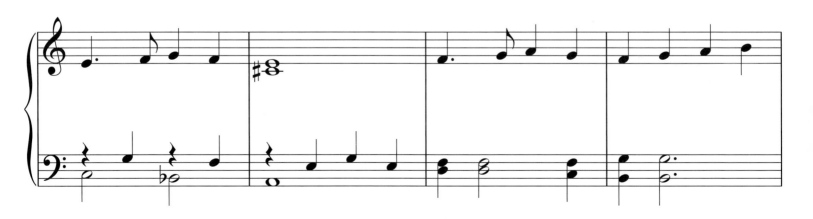

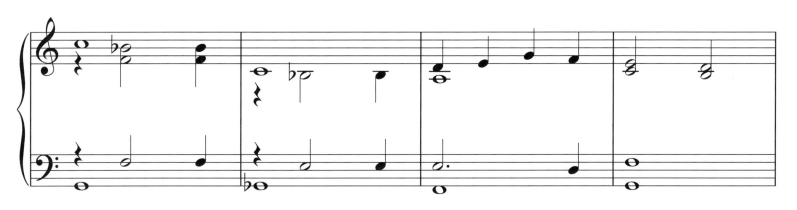

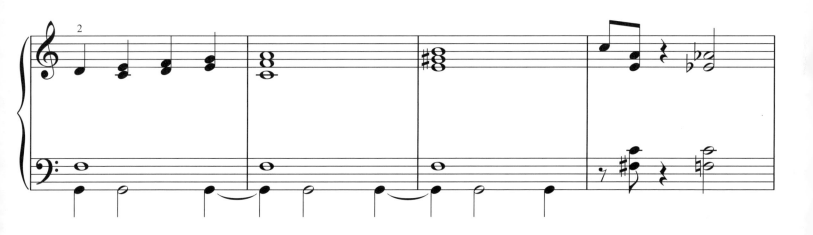

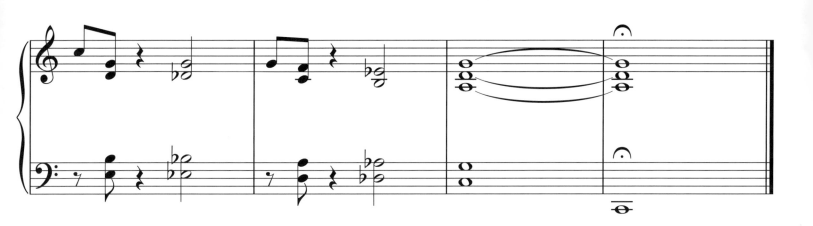

TRÄUMEREI
(Dreaming)
from SCENES FROM CHILDHOOD, OP. 15, NO. 7

By ROBERT SCHUMANN

Slowly, with expression

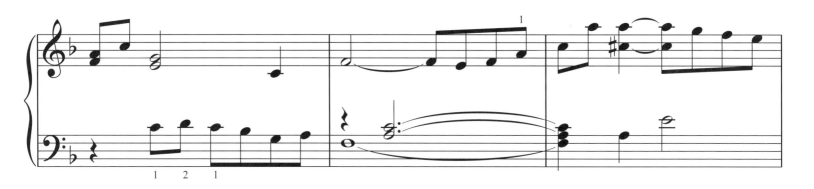

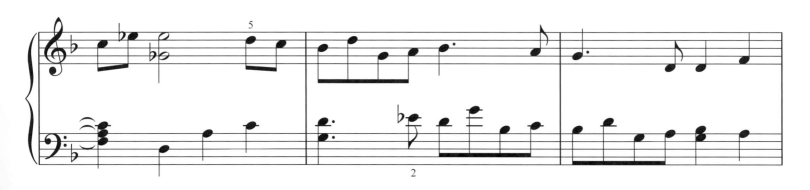

WHEN I FALL IN LOVE
from ONE MINUTE TO ZERO

Words by EDWARD HEYMAN
Music by VICTOR YOUNG

Freely

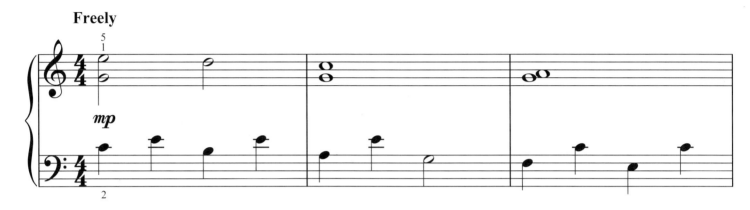